Copyright © 2018 Patrick A. Hegarty.

All rights reserved. No part of this publication may be reproduced, distributed or transmitted in any form or by any means, including photocopying, recording, or other electronic or mechanical methods, without the prior written permission of Patrick Hegarty, except in the case of brief quotations embodied in critical reviews and certain other noncommercial uses permitted by copyright law. For permission requests, email the author, with subject line "Attention: Permissions Enquiry" at the email address below.

admin@spiritandtruth.net.au

www.spiritandtruth.net.au

Scriptures quoted from: New International Version of the Bible. Scripture taken from the Holy Bible, NEW INTERNATIONAL VERSION®. Copyright ©1973, 1978, 1984 International Bible Society. All rights reserved throughout the world. Used by permission of International Bible Society.

Scripture quotations identified MSG are from The Message. Copyright © 1993, 1994, 1995 by Eugene Peterson. Used by permission of NavPress Publishing Group.

Any internet addresses (websites, blogs, etc.) in this book are offered as a resource. They are not intended in any way to be or imply an endorsement by Patrick Hegarty, nor does Patrick Hegarty vouch for the content of these sites for the life of this book.

How to use this material

This manual is designed as a partner to the online training course: Group Facilitator Training, available at www.spiritandtruth.net.au.

RECOMMENDED COURSE FORMAT:

1. Have trainee facilitators watch all the relevant content online prior to meeting together.

2. Each video ends with a response question that should be responded to in this workbook prior to gathering together.

3. Gather all trainee facilitators for a half-day or two evening sessions to process their responses, and focus on any relevant skill development and relationship building.

Contents

Part 1 – Spirit & Truth Groups 1

A unique group setting 1

    Spirit & Truth resources 2

    Stages and movements 3

    Rhythms of grace 5

    Dynamics of transformation 6

    Your part to play in the process 7

    Underlying principles 7

    Spiritual retreat 9

Group meeting culture 10

    Room dynamics 10

    Creating a sense of expectancy 11

    Group agreements 12

Helpful facilitation skills 14

    Ensure each one is heard 14

    Prayer 14

    Go beyond the question and answer method .. 14

    Personality types to be ready for 15

    Working with co-facilitators 16

Part 2 – re:FORM 17

Overview of the course 17

Facilitating week by week 21

    Introductions 21

    Week 1 – How are you doing? 22

    Week 2 – What do you want? 24

    Week 3 - Kairos 26

    Week 4 - Repent 28

    Week 5 - Believe 30

    Week 6 – Walking it out 32

Part 3 – re:FOCUS 34

Overview of the course 34

Facilitating week by week 38

    Introductions 38

    Week 1 – Depth of calling 39

    Week 2 – re:FOCUS on Christ 41

    Week 3 - re:FOCUS on character 43

    Week 4 - re:FOCUS on people 45

    Week 5 - re:FOCUS on talent 47

    Week 6 – re:FOCUS on calling 49

Part 4 – Appendices 51

Group Agreement 51

Co-facilitators 52

Spirit & Truth Groups

A unique group setting

Due to the intensive nature of these courses, and the quite specific and consequential outcomes that are aimed for, it is of great benefit to aim for a special experience of the group-time.

The materials themselves present considerable personal challenge to participants' mindsets and character. They need love, and the presence of God to catalyse significant progress in the discipleship journey.

Effective group facilitation is a vital key to ensuring that the overall journey achieves its goals.

This manual will give you the vital elements you need to play your part.

SPIRIT & TRUTH GROUPS

PERSONAL REFLECTION:

Q. **From Video 1: A unique setting.** What skills, character and knowledge do you have that will help you in this role?

_____

_____

_____

_____

_____

_____

THE SPIRIT & TRUTH RESOURCES

The aim of this suite of materials is to invite people into a deeper, and more vital engagement with God. Every real step of discipleship growth is a step into a more transforming and empowering relationship with Him. The materials are designed play a specific role in that process.

WWW.SPIRITANDTRUTH.NET.AU	
Rhythms of Grace courses	**Training**
Unlocking the Rhythms of Grace Principles of walking & working with God in new ways **re:FORM** Equipping for transformation **re:FOCUS** Discovering true calling	**Group Facilitation** How to lead through the material **Running a great Retreat** Resources to lead a retreat **Prayer Ministry Training** Equipping a ministry team

SPIRIT & TRUTH GROUPS

STAGES AND MOVEMENTS

These materials are short intensives that catalyse movement through key discipleship stages.

As such, they require a higher degree of participation, openness, as well as a desire to change something. Not everyone is prepared to do that, and so participants should be briefed and screened prior to commencement to ensure the whole group is unified in their purpose.

The key stages to navigate are:

Movement 1: Relying on Christ in a new way, and taking steps of obedience – a movement of FAITH.

Movement 2: Creating a preferred future, removing obligation to the old nature – a movement of renewed HOPE.

Movement 3: A desire to bear new fruit, stewarding this life for kingdom purposes – a movement of expressed LOVE.

Even though we need to go through seasons of growth in each area continually, they also play out consecutively in discipleship growth.

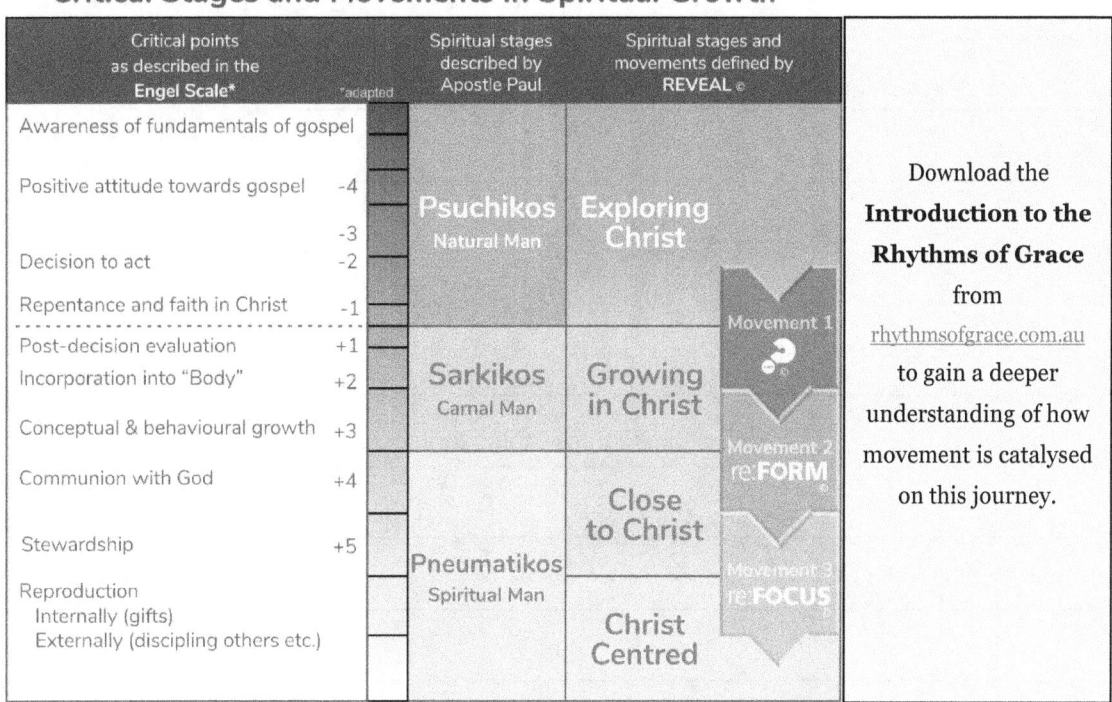

Download the **Introduction to the Rhythms of Grace** from rhythmsofgrace.com.au to gain a deeper understanding of how movement is catalysed on this journey.

Personal Reflection:

Q. **From Video 2: Stages and movements.** At what stage of spiritual maturity do you predominantly dwell? Explain. When and how have you made a significant step forward?

_____
_____
_____
_____
_____
_____
_____
_____
_____
_____
_____
_____
_____
_____
_____
_____
_____
_____
_____
_____
_____

Rhythms of Grace

To grow in the form and function of our life with God, we must change the way we engage with Him. To navigate the movements required we must walk and work in a new way.

> *I'll show you how to take a real rest. Walk with me and work with me—watch how I do it. Learn the unforced rhythms of grace. Mat 11:28-29 (MSG)*

The rhythms each include a step forward to work with God, and a step back to walk with God.

Spirit & Truth: initiates a movement of FAITH (Alpha).

Repent & Believe: initiates a movement of HOPE (re:FORM).

Faith & Deeds: initiating a movement of LOVE (re:FOCUS).

Personal Reflection:

From Video 3: Rhythms of grace.
Q. What form of grace do you draw from God in this season of life? How do you pull back to receive it, and how do you also extend forward to stretch yourself?

_____
_____
_____
_____
_____
_____
_____

Dynamics of transformation

Discipleship growth is a journey that requires four dynamics to be in place:

Relational: By opening up ourselves and joining accountable relationships we become more than we could alone.

Experiential: We need to extend ourselves, developing new habits, and trying new things. Same actions can only produce the same result.

Spiritual: We need to encounter God Himself in new ways, embracing his powerful grace to give us the power we need to change and bear fruit.

Instructional: The truth will set us free. Daily principle-based content that is applied to life through journaled responses is powerful.

Personal Reflection:

From Video 4: Dynamics of transformation.
Q. Which of these four dynamics of transformation are most influential at bringing growth in your life.

_____
_____
_____
_____
_____
_____
_____
_____

Your part to play in the process

As a group facilitator, your role is not to teach. You are to help guide people into these four dynamics. The teaching element is almost completely achieved as the participant reads the content daily and responds honestly.

The group time is a setting where you can help people share, invite God to bring grace, and workshop together to find ways to apply what has been gained.

Each course has a specific outcome. This should be known in advance, so you can ensure the group doesn't drift or dilute in its effectiveness.

Underlying Principles

There are certain foundational principles that are vital to be upheld in our group settings to ensure the effectiveness of the transformation process in this culture.

God is good

Even though our situations, history, and personal wholeness might be devastatingly marred, God is not the author of evil, and is not the Source of our imperfections. We have an enemy who steals, kills and destroys (John 10:10), and it is unhelpful to attribute Satan's works and the effects of the fallen world to our loving Father.

God invites us to life

God's offer to bring life-giving grace where there is death is never removed. Just as He called Simon to become Peter; and Abram to become Abraham – so He continually invites us to greater healing, capacity and impact.

GOD IS ABLE TO REDEEM ANYTHING

Even though God doesn't bring about evil, He is able to take our situation where it is at and bring incredible good from it.

GOD'S GRACE IS ALWAYS AVAILABLE

The promise of totally sufficient grace for every situation is eternal. The forms of grace might be: peace; counsel; joy; healing; wisdom or any number of other ways in which He meets our needs as He sees fit. Our role is to embrace that grace.

WE HONOUR PEOPLE

Our role is not to change people – only God can do that with their cooperation. We are to accept people as they are, honouring their place in the journey they are on, and upholding their dignity at all times.

PERSONAL REFLECTION:

From Video 5: Underlying principles.
Q. What other principles and values would you like to uphold in your group-time?

_____
_____
_____
_____
_____
_____
_____

SPIRITUAL RETREAT

It is highly recommended that a mid-course spiritual retreat be a compulsory part of the program.

Running from Friday evening through to Sunday midday, a retreat allows vital time and space for the participants to pause their normal routine. There they can focus on God alone, and experience many things that can happen much more easily when we immerse ourselves in worship, prayer, personal ministry and practical activities.

The best time to run such a retreat is after the participants have completed two weeks of material.

They can be run at any time, but the impact of the retreat is often so great, and the subsequent openness of the participants so increased, that to delay further is detrimental.

Resources and training on how to conduct a treat are available at the website: www.spiritandtruth.net.au

Group meeting culture

Room Dynamics

It is important to create a group environment that doesn't create obstacles to growth and intimacy.

Leaders should aim to form an accepting, comfortable culture where people can feel heard and understood. It has been said that "*being heard feels so much like being loved that few can tell the difference*". A major goal of group culture is that people do feel loved by God. The ability for people to perceive that love through the Spirit is often made possible by the environment created by His people.

Meetings should be non-judgmental, and absent of advice-giving. If people genuinely need the opinions of others, they should ask specifically.

Whilst acceptance is vital, so is the expectation on the participants to engage fully in the program. Tardiness, sporadic attendance, or lack of genuine sharing sends a message to the rest of the group that the process is not worthwhile, or that the fellow group-members are not valued.

The God-factor:

One of the distinctive and most powerful elements of these programs is the continual and growing invitation for God to speak to and empower the participants. His presence does all the heavy-lifting in regard to transformation.

As such, group-time should be cloaked in prayer, and open to engaging in worship, prayer and personal ministry where appropriate. Group-time is not just about meeting people, but God as well.

Creating a Sense of Expectancy

As we have run these programs over many years, the sheer bulk of testimony about lives changed begins to create a hunger and momentum about registration. The courses fill very quickly when people hear that they will encounter God in some way.

It is quite valuable to build a sense of high anticipation in the participants. If you are new to these materials, you won't have those stories to tell, but there are other great ways to build expectancy among the group.

Fasting:

We have always encouraged our participants to fast from something for the duration of the course. Sometimes it is coffee, or social media, television, or a food group. It is totally up to them.

The great thing about fasting is that the hunger for the thing we abstain from can be converted into a hunger for God Himself. It is a constant reminder that we are in a season of change, and we are reminded to pray.

Worship:

If you have multiple groups meeting at the same venue, start the evening with 30 minutes or so of great worship. You don't need a live band, as video or audio tracks are readily available for use.

Journaling:

We have found great benefit for participants if the facilitator takes time before the first group meeting, to pray for their group members, writing down the prayers and verses God brings to mind. Any insights they might sense God is giving can be included in the journal. This can then be handed to the participants individually.

SPIRIT & TRUTH GROUPS

GROUP AGREEMENTS

The best way to establish the important elements of group culture is through the Group Agreement.

Agreements create group cohesion and buy-in to the process. They define expectations and establish the group norms.

The introductory group session of each course includes time to establish the agreement. The process itself can become a great ice-breaker, and a way of getting to know what is important to each person.

HOW TO CREATE A GROUP AGREEMENT

1. Start with a blank sheet of paper.

2. Write down everything that the participants want on there – but first clarify with them: "What does that mean?" Avoid assumptions

3. If possible write points on a white board- getting the participants to create the group agreement

4. Where possible, address:
    - What is the group time about? What is it not about?
    - Clarify expectations in terms of sharing, participation, teaching
    - Discuss confidentiality- what does it mean for that group?
    - When might confidentiality have to be broken?
    - Discuss the issue of advice giving
    - Attendance and any connection between meetings

5. If necessary, write up the document and give everyone a copy

PERSONAL REFLECTION:

From Video 6: Group Meeting culture

Q. What elements of a group agreement do you believe would be important to emphasis?

_____
_____
_____
_____
_____
_____
_____
_____
_____
_____

Q. What things could do on a weekly basis to enhance the expectancy and dedication to the group setting?

_____
_____
_____
_____
_____
_____
_____
_____
_____
_____

Helpful Facilitation Skills

ENSURE EACH ONE IS HEARD

It is far more important for a group leader to listen, than to speak. We shouldn't feel compelled to offer our own ideas or illustrations unless it serves a clear purpose. Group-time is often too short, and so the most valuable skill is to actually draw out the heart of participants.

PRAYER

Spend time as a group praying for each group member at some point in the course. Also suggest that the group be in prayer for each other through the week, and possibly connecting privately over social media with updates and insights.

BEYOND THE QUESTION & ANSWER METHOD

People become skilled at giving the answer they think we need to hear. But sharing isn't always a sign of an effective meeting. At times you will need to ask follow-up and leading questions that require a deeper response.

Using creative processing such as picture cards, or art & media exercises are great ways for people to explain and express themselves in ways they would never have revealed if simply asked a question.

Other exercises called "Activations" are a way to invite God to prompt the participant in what He is doing and saying in their life. Examples can be found at the back of this book, and the website at www.spiritandtruth.net.au

Personality types to be ready for

Participants aren't perfect, that's why they are in the course. However, group dynamics can often be such that a person might take on a role or type that serves as a defense mechanism to authenticity and accountability.

Some traits to watch out for and manage are:

Emotional: If the perennial crier is let go, other participants often think *"Here we go again, can't we just move on!"*

Long-winded: For this person, the group space is never enough. They're oversharing can shut down others.

The joker: For this person, nothing is ever taken seriously. *"It's not that bad, nothing fazes me"*. Humour is used to avoid real issues.

No-one listens to me: This person buys into powerlessness. *"When is it my turn, no one cares about me, I'm invisible"*

Advice-giver: This expert has been through everything. *"I know what you should do, this is what I did, it's easy"*.

Needy: The attention seeker. If let go too far, other participants close down, or even avoid pre and post group mingling.

Won't share: Getting something out of this person is like pulling teeth. They're disconnection from themselves and others is like an elephant in the room.

Where possible, address any issues that warrant attention privately with the person.

Working with Co-Facilitators

For some courses, particularly re:FORM, there is huge benefit to having a second facilitator on hand. Bedsides the help it provides in the group setting itself, co-facilitation provides a great pathway for new leaders to grow into the facilitator role.

By sharing the load of facilitation through group-time, it gives each facilitator the opportunity to think, pray, and watch the interaction that is taking place.

It is recommended that you spend time with your co-facilitator before the course starts, and perhaps on a weekly basis prior to the next group-time, so you can plan out the session and monitor how each participant is tracking.

You can also share together your own journey as you work through the material. For more information on meeting with your co-facilitator, see the appendix section at the back of this manual.

Personal Reflection:

From Video 7: Helpful facilitation skills

Q. Recall a time when a difficult personality interrupted a group meeting. What did you learn, and how did you respond?

_____

_____

_____

_____

_____

_____

re:FORM

Overview of the course

re:FORM equips participants with the life-long skill of how to partner with God in transformation and spiritual growth.

Using a very simple circular process, participants learn to identify the fruit and symptoms of harmful beliefs and emotional pain.

They then bring those aspects to the cross, and actively rely on God to provide the grace needed to journey towards a God-honouring preferred future.

RE:FORM

At its heart, re:FORM enables disciples to navigate the movement from being essentially carnal, to spiritual. Paul defines these two stages in 1 Corinthians 2:14 – 3:1, in particular by saying:

> *I could not address you as people who live by the Spirit (Gk: pneumatikos - spiritual) but as people who are still worldly (Gk: sarkikos - carnal)—mere infants in Christ.*

This is a key movement in discipleship, since so many have no concept of how to life from the Spirit of Christ within.

The entire course revolves around the single verse: Mark 1:15:

> *"The time (Gk: kairos) has come," he said. "The kingdom of God has come near. Repent and believe the good news!"*

Participants are equipped to recognize these Kairos moments, and take a detour off their normal reactionary path into a profound expression of repentance and belief. They can then re-enter their life better equipped to cut-off carnal behavior.

re:FORM

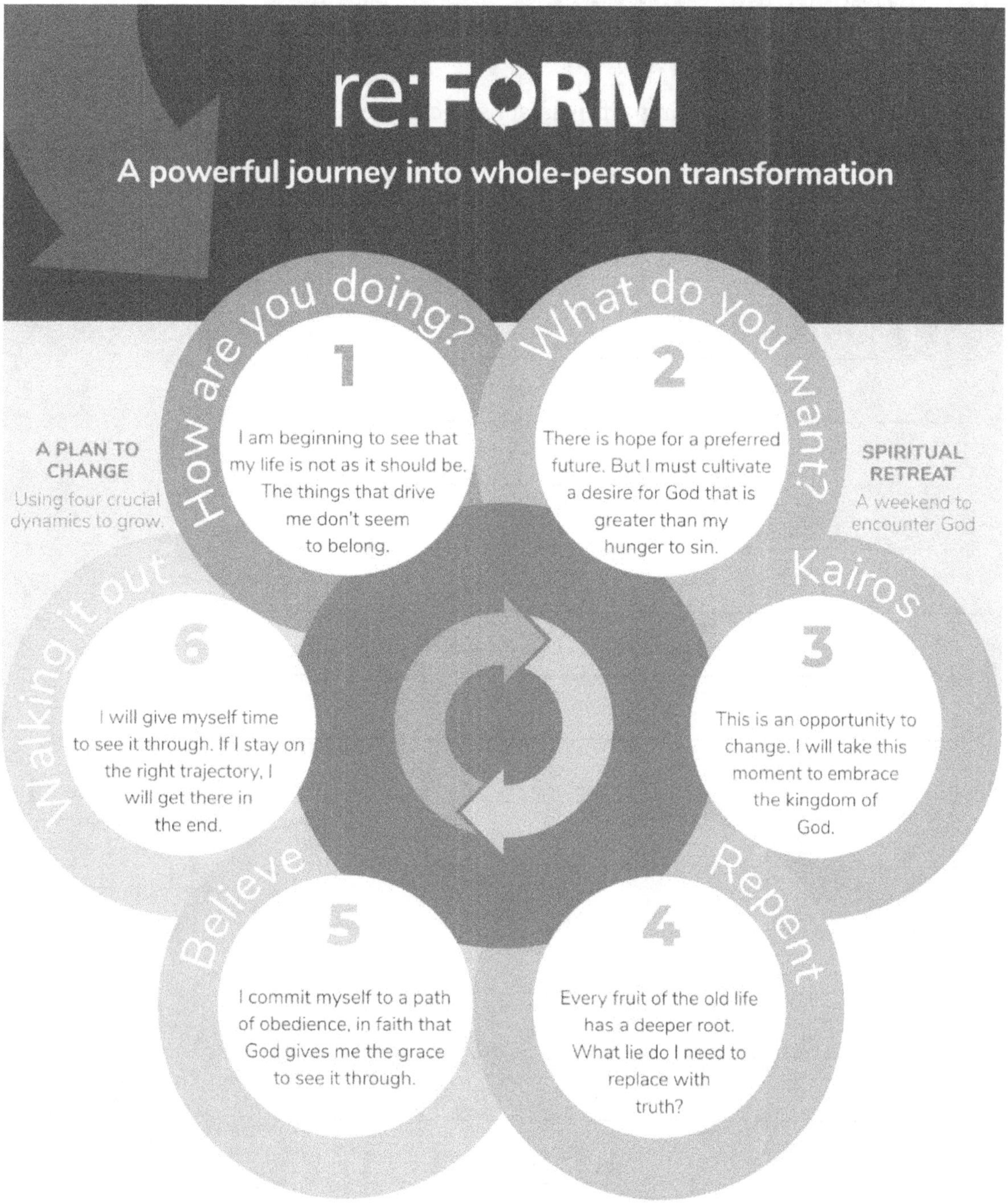

re:FORM
A powerful journey into whole-person transformation

A PLAN TO CHANGE
Using four crucial dynamics to grow.

1 — How are you doing?
I am beginning to see that my life is not as it should be. The things that drive me don't seem to belong.

2 — What do you want?
There is hope for a preferred future. But I must cultivate a desire for God that is greater than my hunger to sin.

SPIRITUAL RETREAT
A weekend to encounter God

3 — Kairos
This is an opportunity to change. I will take this moment to embrace the kingdom of God.

4 — Repent
Every fruit of the old life has a deeper root. What lie do I need to replace with truth?

5 — Believe
I commit myself to a path of obedience, in faith that God gives me the grace to see it through.

6 — Walking it out
I will give myself time to see it through. If I stay on the right trajectory, I will get there in the end.

A circular journey of repentance and belief

Jesus invites us to embrace the power of the kingdom of God at specific moment, and for specific things. "The time has come," he said. "The kingdom of God has come near. Repent and believe the good news!" **Mark 1:15**

re:FORM equips people to identify and address areas of their life that need transformation. They then turn from them, learning how to embrace the grace of Christ to live differently.

PERSONAL REFLECTION:

From Video 8: re:FORM

Q. What has been the most impacting lessons or changes that re:FORM has been part of in your own life?

_____

_____

_____

_____

_____

_____

_____

_____

_____

_____

_____

_____

_____

_____

_____

_____

_____

_____

_____

_____

_____

_____

_____

RE:FORM

Facilitating Week by Week

INTRODUCTIONS

GROUP MEETING 1

The goal of this meeting is to essentially set the tone for the rest of the course.

In this meeting the facilitator should provide the necessary framework for the course in regard to:

- Daily readings and journal responses.
- How to use the separate workbook.
- Importance of the weekly group-time.
- Attendance of the mid-course retreat.

Participants are introduced to each other, invited to share their story, and lay out what they hope to experience from the six-week journey.

Their expectations may or may-not be valid or particularly deep at this point, but that can be discussed, or else you simply let the journey itself challenge their hopes.

It is important that this first meeting include a time of setting up a group agreement that every participant has buy-in with.

The various questions included in the material can be asked as required, but there will probably not be enough time to go through them all.

Ensure the meeting is concluded with a time of prayer where everyone is ministered too, and each participant encouraged to pray.

RE:FORM

WEEK 1 – HOW ARE YOU DOING?

Comparing our present life against God's ideal.

The focus of week 1 is to invite the participants to enter the journey of transformation from the dysfunction and powerlessness that they currently experience, into the offer of abundant life God can give.

Highlighting areas such as fear and pride, the week concludes by offering hope that God can and will bring change to a life that hungers for it.

1.1 **Come to life** – ours is a half-life if we are not living from God's Spirit.
1.2 **Called** – God is developing us into the fulfillment of the name He has given us.
1.3 **What owns you?** – Our personal slave-drivers keep us locked in our old nature.
1.4 **Afraid and alone** – An orphaned spirit turns to idols rather than our Father God.
1.5 **Corrupted comparison** – pride and conceit fuel much of our action and ambition.
1.6 **Redeemed hope** – when our mind is set on what can and should be we can't help but aim for it.

GROUP MEETING 2

This meeting focusses on defining the areas in which God has (or would like to) address in the participants' lives.

The Spiritual Health Assessment is a helpful tool for ensuring each one can identify an area of life in which to focus the principles of the course.

Ensure some time is spent fleshing out what a preferred future might look like for each participant.

RE:FORM

Helpful hints

This session will hopefully be one of frank transparency. Whilst it may be a challenge, and very new for some people to open up, encourage them that this is a special season and environment for them where God is working on the inner world of everyone.

Often it helps if one participant takes initiative to demonstrate heart-felt and appropriate levels of transparency to the group, as it gives permission to the others to be vulnerable as well.

If none step forward, then one of the facilitators might need to articulate what God is dealing with in their own life.

_____
_____
_____
_____
_____
_____
_____
_____
_____
_____
_____
_____
_____
_____
_____
_____
_____
_____
_____
_____

RE:FORM

Week 2 – What do you want?

Creating a preferred future for my life

The second week is a vital step in the process of change. If people lack the will or hunger to grow, they won't. The content and questions seek to give the participant a desire for God as well as the life He offers.

2.1 **Out of the box** – Jesus wants to break us out of the constrained ways we see ourselves and our circumstance.

2.2 **The posture of hope** – Jesus encourages those who seek life to pursue humility and a desire to for God.

2.3 **Building desire** – Our passions should be fueled by what we value and commit to, not what our old-nature demands.

2.4 **Desiring God** – Our love for God Himself is to be the priority and fuel for all we do.

2.5 **Desiring freedom** – To break free from bondage, you have to want it.

2.6 **Creating a hope** – Can you dream for something beyond your present experience?

Group meeting 3

After having the participants reflect on their responses to the daily content, help them form up the basics of a preferred future using the table and questions provided in the notes.

re:FORM

Helpful hints

This is meeting preferably precedes your spiritual retreat. Brief the participants on what to expect, and how to prepare spiritually.

They should:

- Try where possible to remove stress and arrive in a peaceful and expectant frame of mind.
- Commit to being at the whole retreat – any absence greatly effects the impact.
- Come committed to press in to God personally, and to worship in the midst of their circumstance.
- Remove expectations on God as to what they want Him to do in their life.
- Be prepared to deal with anything God sovereignly chooses to raise with them.

Week 3 – Kairos

Recognising areas that God can change.

In this week of content, the participants begin to take the circular journey of transformation. Having cultivated a degree of desire in preceding weeks, and having hopefully completed their spiritual retreat, they should be in a position to openness and surrender.

3.1 **What time is it?** – When we become aware of a harmful reaction it is an opportune moment to change.

3.2 **One more night** – Avoiding the issue only exacerbates it.

3.3 **Spotting the problem** – What might seem inconsequential to us, could be a major issue for God.

3.4 **Approaching the no-go zone** – There are some issues we avoid dealing with at almost any cost.

3.5 **What is the alternative?** – Our own strength can't beat sin – we need God's help.

3.6 **Placing everything on the table** – To be totally free there must be nothing left to hide.

Group meeting 4

Begin the meeting by spending time reflecting on the experiences and lessons learned from those who attended a spiritual retreat.

As you process the participant's responses to this week's content, recognize that it is a potentially difficult moment in their journey.

Some will have been confronted with issues they have ignored or felt defeated in for many years. Others will have many new questions following on from a spiritual retreat.

RE:FORM

HELPFUL HINTS

Following on from the spiritual retreat participants are potentially dealing with a spectrum of responses, such as:

- I am astounded. I will never doubt God again after what He showed me.
- I am disappointed, I expected God to do a certain thing, and it never happened. There is no hope for me.
- I am offended! People did and said things that I don't like or agree with.

At this moment we need to pastorally care for the participants, and set them up for positive next-steps.

Remind participants that:

- Every person's experience and journey is different, and we should not compare.
- God does in us what He needs to, and is allowed to do, in each of us. We all have a different clock we are working to with Him.
- Don't assume there are different levels to our experience of God or spiritual gifting – otherwise we devalue some and elevate others. This was the Corinthian problem.
- Our goal is to engage with and worship God personally. Whatever we do or do not experience is up to Him.

_____
_____
_____
_____
_____
_____
_____
_____

RE:FORM

WEEK 4 – REPENT

Turning from lies and adopting God's truth.

The reason we remain stuck in our dysfunction is that we do not know how to navigate repentance comprehensively. By identifying the bad fruit in our life, we can easily become experts in saying sorry, while experiencing no change.

Jesus calls us in to a partnership where we faithfully do what we can in our own strength, in faith that He will help us live in godly ways.

- 4.1 **A rhythm of grace** – Transformation is not about trying harder, but of walking and working with God.
- 4.2 **Repentance** – We don't just turn away from one thing, we turn towards something better.
- 4.3 **Looking behind the idol** – All bad fruit finds its source in a bad root.
- 4.4 **Dishonour** – As a child we learn to dishonor, robbing us of the blessing we need.
- 4.5 **Offence** – We are only free when we can clear the scales of judgment.
- 4.6 **Navigating a turn** – Saying sorry does nothing, repentance makes a choice to change.

GROUP MEETING 5

The process of looking deeper for the root of dysfunction will probably be a new process for most participants. Not everyone will find it easy. Ask each one to share as they feel comfortable in that setting.

Remember, no advice giving! Facilitators are not authorized counsellors or therapists. We can however ask questions that might help identify where wrong thinking or judgements began.

RE:FORM

HELPFUL HINTS

The two major issues of dishonour and offence were raised in this week's content. Of course, there are many other areas of significant dysfunction in our lives beyond these two. And it is doubtful that participants would have seen them as an issue at the beginning of the course.

However, these two issues are rooted in judgment, an issue that Jesus clearly stated and demonstrated cuts us off from the blessing of God that we would normally enjoy.

Historical unforgiveness and bitterness towards others is a factor in the huge majority of spiritual dysfunctions.

If your participants have recognized this in their own lives then help them process that by leading them in specific prayers of repentance. Also ensure that is followed up with a clear declaration of forgiveness (John 20:23)

_____
_____
_____
_____
_____
_____
_____
_____
_____
_____
_____
_____
_____
_____

Week 5 – Believe

Relying on God to do what we never could

The type of faith that helps us profoundly overcome, is one that is above the circumstances. Regardless of our past or present circumstance, we rely on the fact that God gives us what we need.

This week's content challenged participants in how to find peace, rest and joy in the presence of God alone.

5.1 **The kingdom is at hand** – Faith is an active reliance on the provision of God
5.2 **What storm?** – Faith doesn't mean the seas are always calm, but that we can be calm in any seas.
5.3 **The rest of faith** – God knows what we need and provides when we need it – that's His job.
5.4 **Pathway to joy** – Faith brings peace, and peace leaves us with joy.
5.5 **The higher calling** – Kingdom life brings access to an inheritance of influence.
5.6 **A point of no return** – true steps of faith require us to delete any potential exit strategy.

Group meeting 6

One of the great challenges for immature believers to embrace is the idea of having faith in God through the circumstance, rather than faith that He will (and is in some way obliged to) make our life easier.

Work the various questions and responses through with the participants with a mind to finding satisfaction in who God is, rather than what He does.

RE:FORM

HELPFUL HINTS

To be able to live *from* God's provision, through His Spirit, is probably the single most important skill believers need to master. We need to extend less energy trying harder to be good, and more energy engaging with His unlimited grace. It is not a skill that comes naturally to our fallen, independent minds.

The key is knowing how to "turn" to Jesus. It means we look away from sin, and look to Him in adoration and in trust.

You may want to have the group read 2 Corinthians 3:16-18, which articulates this transformation from glory to glory as we gaze upon God.

Then workshop together how that can be applied in their context of needing God to provide. If they need peace, or strength or wisdom etc. then pray with them that God would provide it, and encourage them to rely on that provision.

RE:FORM

Week 6 – Walking it out

Creating a plan to change

We don't change simply by talking about it or waiting. We need to make a plan and take a step or two. This week the participants were walked through the four dynamics of change, and encouraged to fill out their Plan to Change.

6.1 **What am I aiming for really?** – God's aim is to have your heart, what is yours?

6.2 **Walking in Union** – You can only give what you genuinely possess.

6.3 **Heart of flesh; face like flint** – We must stay both soft to God, and resolute to follow Him.

6.4 **How did Jesus grow people?** – With the dynamics of transformation, growth in any area is possible.

6.5 **Form a strategy** – These four layers of connection will transform your life.

6.6 **Take a step** – It is time to get started.

Group meeting 7

When having the participants share their Plan to Change with the group, keep an eye out for ways to ensure they know when they are succeeding. The key point in each section of the plan is "I will know when I am succeeding when ..."

They need to find ways to measure progress, otherwise it becomes an undefined set of intentions that have no accountability.

RE:FORM

HELPFUL HINTS

At this point, some groups and people will want and need to meet again to continue the journey they have just begun.

Facilitators may or may-not find it suitable to do that, but it can be helpful to meet again from time-to-time to encourage each other's journey.

Recommend that they all have accountability partners in place.

Suggest also that they complete another Plan to Change from time to time, as a discipline through life.

A simple download of the Plan to Change is available at the website www.spiritandtruth.net.au

re:FOCUS

Overview of the course

re:FOCUS is a course for those who are ready to steward their life for the purposes of God. This major phase of discipleship growth follows that of becoming spiritually mature in Christ.

Dangers face those who want to sacrificially and humbly give their time and talent to God. Many only know a functionary lifestyle where it is all about doing.

But doing flows from being. We need to know who we are, and where we fit in the grand plans of God, since our path lies within His.

re:FOCUS

re:FOCUS emphasizes form-over-function in regard to discovery of calling. God is much more interested in how you relate to Him, and the people around you, than He is about what you do for Him.

The general flow of the course begins with a call to consider the true depth of our calling in Christ. Our vision gets blurred by the bombardment of priorities and noise of our current worl, and so we must re:FOCUS.

The course then brings us back to a grander vision for life, centred around and fueled by our walk with God. Spending a week on each of the following themes:

re:FOCUS on Christ – prioritizing union with God.

re:FOCUS on Character – cultivating who I am becoming.

re:FOCUS on People – influencing those around me.

re:FOCUS on Talent – giving it everything I have got.

re:FOCUS on Calling – having a plan to re:FOCUS.

At the end of the course, participants will have completed a Plan to re:FOCUS, detailing goals they may have to ensure their calling is kept on track.

At its heart, re:FOCUS emphasises the rhythm of grace we call Faith & Deeds. This symbiotic relationship assumes we rely on God to bear the fruit we long for, but that we must also play our part in obedience, making room for God to work through us.

re:FOCUS

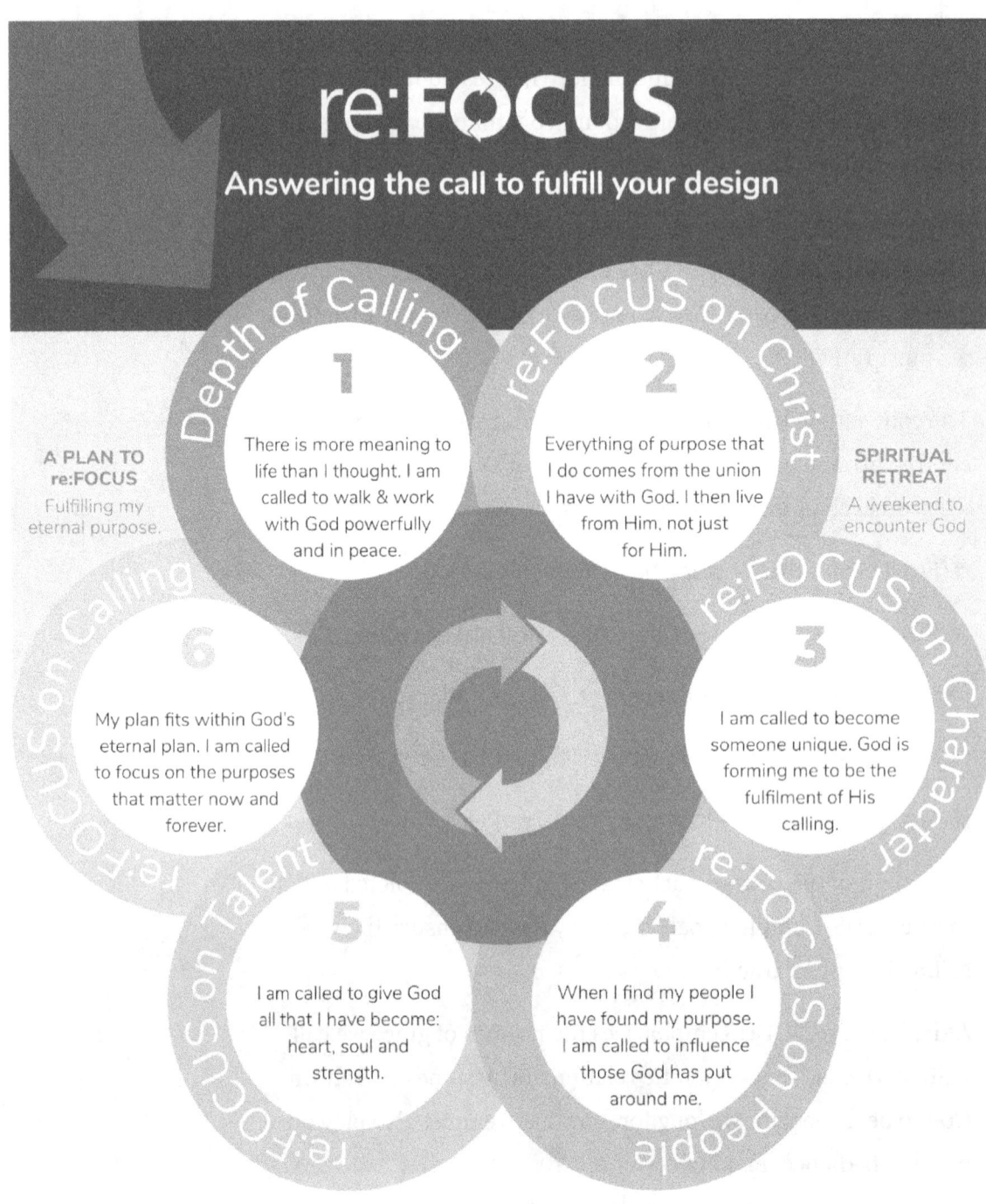

A life of purpose and fruitfulness requires faith & deeds

The world bombards us with priorities and distractions that blur our vision. We need to rediscover why we exist, and how that applies to life on this time and place.

re:FOCUS helps participants to realign their thinking and actions with eternal calling and design. But real impact comes from the power of Christ within, and so we must learn how to partner with Christ if we are to bear eternal fruit.

PERSONAL REFLECTION:

From Video 9: re:FOCUS

Q. How do you define what God's calling is on your life? Who has he formed you to be? Who are the people you are called to invest in? What talent mix has he entrusted to you?

Facilitating Week by Week

INTRODUCTIONS

GROUP MEETING 1

The goal of this meeting is to essentially set the tone for the rest of the course.

In this meeting the facilitator should provide the necessary framework for the course in regard to:

- Daily readings and journal responses.
- How to use the separate workbook.
- Importance of the weekly group-time.
- Attendance of the mid-course retreat.

Participants are introduced to each other, invited to share their story, and lay out what they hope to experience from the six-week journey.

Their expectations may or may-not be valid or particularly deep at this point, but that can be discussed, or else you simply let the journey itself challenge their hopes.

It is important that this first meeting include a time of setting up a group agreement that every participant has buy-in with.

The various questions included in the material can be asked as required, but there will probably not be enough time to go through them all.

Ensure the meeting is concluded with a time of prayer where everyone is ministered too, and each participant encouraged to pray.

re:FOCUS

Week 1 – Depth of calling

The call to walk and work with God

The focus of week 1 is to reveal both the shallowness of ambition without God, and the depth of purpose we find with Him.

The key to fulfilling calling is to engage with Him, drawing from His power as we step out in faith and obedience.

1.1 **Depth of calling** – You are called to something deeper than merely doing.
1.2 **The need to re:FOCUS** – We need God's help and perspective to see our calling as we should.
1.3 **Impressive or impacting** – Which legacy will we choose
1.4 **Life in God's garden** – To understand God's plan for you, we must go back to the beginning.
1.5 **Walking and working in the garden** – We are called to faith and deeds that are fueled by our relationship with God.
1.6 **The relational rhythm** – Living from our own strength is only part of our potential story.

Group meeting 2

The content from week one challenges much of what we have been doing and why. The idea of living from God's strength, whilst being attractive, is also allusive to most people.

In the group time, try to emphasise the participants own stories of when they have seen God do something through them, even in a small way. Partnering with God is a skill that takes time and grows with practice. Small wins should be celebrated as much as big ones.

RE:FOCUS

HELPFUL HINTS

Depending on how discussion is going, some extra questions you could in this session are:

Q. How balanced would you say you have been in seeking God's presence and communion, compared to wanting to know what He wants you to do?

Q. Are you able to identify areas of your life where you are more interested in impressing people, than impacting them? Why would that be?

Q. Talk together about your own experiences of forming a vision for a God-centred life, ministry or vocation. Did it go to plan?

Q. Are you more of a walker or a worker? Talk together about how that does or doesn't work out well for you and those around you.

Q. How do you most easy relate to God:

- As a child who finds rest, healing, security and acceptance with the heavenly Father?
- Or, as an heir who wants to do things that matter, even at great personal expense?

_____
_____
_____
_____
_____
_____
_____
_____
_____

Week 2 – re:FOCUS on Christ

Knowing Whose I am

Week 2 has brought the focus of life back to its barest element, communion with God. Rather than looking at what we can do for Him, we focus first on who we are because of Him, and what that means for us practically.

2.1 **First** – Our commitment to serve God cannot outstrip our communion with Him.
2.2 **Getting derailed** – Asking the questions: Who am I, and Whose am I?
2.3 **Abiding** – Only by dwelling deeply and continually with God do we bear kingdom fruit that lasts.
2.4 **Changing lenses** – To embrace our next upgrade, we must change our view of what is possible.
2.5 **re:FOCUS on Christ** – When we look away from Christ, we become practical atheists.
2.6 **Living from Christ** – As we build our faith through intimacy, we can't help but do extraordinary deeds.

GROUP MEETING 3

It is easy for mature Christians to nod their head at the idea of having a more profound union with Christ. We tend to think we have this area covered and want to move on.

The reality is, if our communion with God is where it should be, we don't need to ask many questions about life direction and calling.

Ensure participants reflect deeply on whether their walk with God is as it should be by His standards, not theirs.

RE:FOCUS

HELPFUL HINTS

Depending on how discussion is going, some extra questions you could in this session are:

Q. How or why might you have lost your first love for Christ?

Q. Some of what is done in God's name, even within churches, can seem fueled by wrong ambitions. What do you think would change in the priorities of church life generally, if God's people were more deeply connected with Christ?

Q. What do you think John 5:19 means when Jesus says: "*The Son can do nothing by himself; he can do only what he sees his Father doing*"?

- How would Jesus see what the Father was doing?
- Do you believe this a lifestyle that we can and should be able to emulate to some extent? If so, how might we take further steps in this?

Q. What can you learn about yourself and God from the miracles that you have seen Him do in the past?

Q. How have you fallen in to the trap of practical atheism in your life?

_____
_____
_____
_____
_____
_____
_____
_____
_____
_____

Week 3 – re:FOCUS on character

Cultivating who I am becoming

When it comes to embracing what God is trying to accomplish in us, it is who we are becoming that matters. What we do springs from who we are. This week, participants are encouraged to look at the person God is forming them to be.

3.1 **I have made you** – Calling is less about what you achieve, and more about who you become.
3.2 **Stuck in a moment** – Our next step of guidance may well depend on our obedience to the previous one.
3.3 **Growing character** – When all forms of supply are cut off except God Himself – we turn to Him more deeply, and grow like Him more fully.
3.4 **The fruit of perseverance** – From our worst of circumstance God plans to bring the fruit of hope.
3.5 **The wilderness effect** – Our wilderness is designed to draw us to God – lest we find ourselves in a desert.
3.6 **re:FOCUS on character** – Destiny is never focused on the outcome, but the way we take the journey.

Group meeting 4

Most people will quickly relate to having wilderness seasons in their life, remembering the pain and frustration of that.

Spend time drawing out the gold of those experiences, encouraging group members to see the unending purpose God is building, and the great fruit that is coming from the process.

Hear their stories, and help identify the subsequent fruit.

re:FOCUS

Helpful hints

Depending on how discussion is going, some extra questions you could in this session are:

Q. Think back over recent seasons of your life, mindful of some of the lessons God has been teaching you. What has He been building in to your life that is forming you as a person?

Q. Did you cooperate with that process, or might you have hampered it in some way through your choices or responses?

Q. Are there habits, mindsets, traditions, and relationship dynamics from your childhood that hold you back?

Q. Have you ever found yourself "fighting against the tide" of God's dealings in your life? He may have been initiating a retreat when you are pushing for advance, or vice-versa. How would you describe that season? Did you finally begin to cooperate with God in His ways?

Q. Share with each other in the group, the ways you are able to embrace and apply the Lord's strength through your difficult times.

Q. How have you been transformed by the wilderness seasons of your life?

Q. Is there any way you could have drawn benefit from a wilderness season more quickly or more deeply?

_____
_____
_____
_____
_____
_____
_____
_____

WEEK 4 – RE:FOCUS ON PEOPLE

Influencing those around me

This week the participants are encouraged to see the people around them as the primary ministry area for life. Rather that looking for the next project or assignment from God, we should look first at those people we already have responsibility to impact.

4.1 **People are your purpose** – When you find your people you have found your purpose.
4.2 **Your area of influence** – God has assigned you a boundary in which you have authority to impact.
4.3 **You and the church** – To find the fullness of God's calling on your life, you also need to find yourself in church.
4.4 **Oikos – those you do life with** – Your greatest calling is to those who are closest to you.
4.5 **Your tribe** – We find unreasonable allegiance from those who wear the same colours.
4.6 **re:FOCUS on people** – God needs to be the centre of our life and present in all our relationships.

GROUP MEETING 5

At times we feel we want to achieve something in life, but people seem to keep getting in the way. Wrong! People aren't the problem, they are the purpose.

Nor are people projects that we can take on with a view to having them reach a certain point. Again, people aren't a means to an end, they are the end itself.

In your group time, help the participants see the immense value and priority of the people God has given.

RE:FOCUS

HELPFUL HINTS

Depending on how discussion is going, some extra questions you could in this session are:

Q. If our purpose is to bring grace to people, what implications does that have (if any) on your current situation at work, home and school? How do you see those situations being used or changed by God?

Q. Are you more people-oriented, or are you task-oriented? How does affect your ability and desire to minister to people regularly?

Q. If you could define it, how would you describe the unique part God has equipped you to be in the church?

Q. Is there anything about your tribes, past or present, that was not helpful to your Christian calling?

Q. Where has been your greatest area of influence with God's help? How do you determine that?

_____
_____
_____
_____
_____
_____
_____
_____
_____
_____
_____
_____
_____

Week 5 – re:FOCUS on talent

Giving it everything I have got

This week's content looks at the wealth of resources God has put in our hands to use for His purpose. It encourages participants to invest maximum effort of heart, soul and strength into God's will for their life.

5.1 **re:FOCUS on talent** – We all have a portfolio of God-given resources to invest in the kingdom.

5.2 **Put your soul into it** – Being faithful in your calling is about investing who you are into the very few things in life that matters.

5.3 **The heart speaks** – Your core values determine what you will and won't stand for.

5.4 **The need at hand** – When looking for your calling, look first to what the world actually needs.

5.5 **Spiritual gifts** – Your spiritual gifts bring God-sized fruit from your work with Him.

5.6 **When doing to for God isn't enough** – Trying to fulfill God's will without sticking to God's plan can leave us high and dry.

GROUP MEETING 6

At this point in a discussion of life-direction, people like to use various personality profiles and spiritual gift assessments to get a handle on their strengths and weaknesses.

Feel free to recommend any such tools that come from a reputable source. Suggested links can be found on the website at www.spiritandtruth.net.au

RE:FOCUS

HELPFUL HINTS

Depending on how discussion is going, some extra questions you could in this session are:

Q. Which tendency comes most naturally to you: to focus on using and growing your strengths; or to focus on fixing your weaknesses? Explain why.

Q. What talents are you intentionally investing in God's work?

Q. How is your emotional life going in regard to God's calling? Are you excited; exhausted; frustrated; or focused?

Q. How could you adjust your life to bring greater emphasis of time and resources into the things that matter?

Q. What are the things that stop us from looking first to the needs at hand when determining our calling?

Q. Share with the group a time when having faith in God changed the way you had been approaching a situation.

_____
_____
_____
_____
_____
_____
_____
_____
_____
_____
_____
_____

WEEK 6 – RE:FOCUS ON CALLING

Creating a Plan to re:FOCUS

The goal of this final week is to complete a helpful Plan to re:FOCUS. By looking at the broader aspects of God's eternal plan, and eight clear purpose statements, participants can create some simple goals to ensure they stay on track.

6.1 **re:FOCUS on calling** – Your purpose is found within God's greater purpose.
6.2 **Purpose: Get back to the garden** – God has given specific mandates with which to pursue His calling.
6.3 **Whose am I?** – You are God's child and Christ's co-heir. Let that refocus your vision.
6.4 **Who am I becoming?** – You are called to be who Christ would be if Christ were you.
6.5 **Who are mine?** – Your greatest impact comes from loving and leading people.
6.6 **What have I got?** – All that you are, and all you have been given, only reach their potential when they are laid down for God to use.

GROUP MEETING 7

Invest the majority of group-time in working through the participant's Plan to re:FOCUS. Ensure any goals have measurable outcomes that motivate.

As a final check for validity of the plans, revise the four mandates of session 6.2 to ensure that there is sufficient balance of intention there.

re:FOCUS

HELPFUL HINTS

At this point, some groups and people will want and need to meet again to continue the journey they have just begun.

Facilitators may or may-not find it suitable to do that, but it can be helpful to meet again from time-to-time to encourage each other's journey.

Recommend that they all have accountability partners in place.

Suggest also that they complete another Plan to re:FOCUS from time to time, as a discipline through life.

A simple download of the Plan to re:FOCUS is available at the website www.spiritandtruth.net.au

Appendix 1 – Group Agreement

GROUP ATTENDANCE

We will honour each other by being on time and regularly attending meetings.

SAFE ENVIRONMENT

We will create a place where each person is protected and loved, free to share without judgment or unsolicited advice.

RESPECT DIFFERENCES

We will be gentle and gracious to those with different spiritual maturity, opinions and temperaments.

CONFIDENTIALITY

What is said in the group stays in the group.

FAITHFULNESS

We will diligently engage with the material, processing our responses honestly.

OTHER POINTS OF IMPORTANCE TO YOU

_____

_____

_____

_____

Signed

_____   _____

_____   _____

_____   _____

Appendix 2 - Co-facilitators

When you have your first meeting with your co-facilitator these are a few points that might be helpful to discuss. Both facilitators share their answers.

Q. Why are you a Steps leader?

Q. Sharer you experience of previous group facilitation. What was good? What was hard?

Q. What do you bring to the partnership?

- What are your gifts?
- What are your strengths and limitations?
- What do you find hard when leading?
- What do you find rewarding and life giving?

Q. What do you expect of your co-facilitator?

- What does shared load and responsibility look like?
- What do you need from me?

Q. How do you like to facilitate?

- Do you tend to be structured in your approach or do you prefer to let the session flow spontaneously?
- Are you comfortable to draw participants out to share at a deeper level?
- Do you enjoy teaching?
- How do you like to add prayer and ministry to the session?
- How comfortable are you with creative processes?

Q. What areas of co-facilitation do you want to grow in? How can I help?

APPENDICES

GUIDELINES FOR CO-FACILITATION

BEFORE THE GROUP

- Schedule a time for planning
- Take time to get to know each other
- Discuss each other's style of planning and facilitating
- Avoid making assumptions about one another
- Take time to talk through your Steps journey
- Discuss any concerns/potential challenges
- Ensure the session themes are clear
- Discuss any triggers
- Plan ways to give signals to one another
- Divide introduction of activities fairly
- Schedule a time after the workshop to debrief

DURING THE GROUP

- Keep communicating with each other throughout the group
- Support and validate one another
- Be flexible
- Include your co-facilitator even when you are leading an exercise or discussion, by asking, for example: "Do you have anything to add?"
- Use lots of eye contact
- Remember that it's okay to make mistakes
- Take the initiative to step in if your co-facilitator misses an opportunity to address a point
- Keep track of time

AFTER THE GROUP

- Confirm time for debrief meeting
- Listen carefully to one another's assessment of the session
- Discuss what worked well and what didn't

APPENDICES

- Brainstorm what could have been done differently
- Name particular behaviours, for example: "When you kept interrupting me, I felt undermined and frustrated", or "I got the impression that some participants were bored"
- Realize the importance and potential difficulty of debriefing a challenging session

Notes:

Notes:

Notes:

Notes:

www.ingramcontent.com/pod-product-compliance
Lightning Source LLC
Chambersburg PA
CBHW081421300426
44110CB00017BA/2342